The Movie Script

How to Write a Screenplay

Tomas Sorensen

TS Publishing

CONTENTS

DEAR READER

Thanks a lot for purchasing this book

I really hope it will inspire you on your screenwriting and filmmaking journey. This book is for all filmmakers, newcomers, students and established industry professionals seeking more knowledge. The main idea behind the publication of the screenplay for my short film "The Unhappy Woman" is to show you how a screenplay is written, how the plotting works, and how the dialogue is implemented. I hope it will give you some creative input regardless of what kind of movie you're working on – a short film, feature film, or documentary.

Please read the script carefully, analyze it, and watch the film. That's the best way to learn. Two different screenplay versions are available—one easy-to-read version in Chapter 4 and one correctly formatted version in Chapter 5. In Chapter 5, there are links to the various sources for watching the film.

Enjoy!

1

GET INSPIRED

Dear film enthusiast

I sincerely hope the screenplay for "The Unhappy Woman" will inspire you to accomplish your next movie project. My little film went on a great journey, culminating in an amazing win at the Aspen Shortsfest—one of the world's leading short film events! "The Movie Script – How to Write a Screenplay" is a short guide to the most important step in the wonderful filmmaking process: writing the screenplay!

Here, you have the opportunity to read the English version of "The Unhappy Woman. The film was originally written and filmed in Norwegian and later translated into English. By reading and analyzing the screenplay you will surely get the tools you need on the way to write scripts for your future film projects.

"The Unhappy Woman" was written, directed, produced, and edited by the undersigned. The film premiered in 2009 and did very well at several renowned festivals. In 2010, it won one of the main prizes at the Aspen Shortsfest, where it was awarded the Best Short Short Award, which is given to films up to five minutes long. This Oscar-eligible award led to the film's submission for consideration for an Academy Award nomination. Other film festivals with "The Unhappy Woman" on the poster were the Palm Springs Film Fest, the Boulder International Film Festival, the Norwegian Short Film Festival in Grimstad, and several others. Later, the project received worldwide digital distribution on several streaming platforms.

This is a simple film—very simple—two actors in a corridor and a crew of six. The budget was nearly nothing, and we filmed everything we needed in under two hours. The filming was intense and great fun, thanks to our two wonderful actors, Henriette Steenstrup and John Brungot. They delivered brilliant performances and were very engaged in the project.

I really felt we worked together as a team on this project. Everyone was eager to make the best possible film to make the story work. The precise story carries the movie. American star actress Meg Ryan was the head of the jury during the 2010 Aspen Shortsfest. Her description of "The Unhappy Woman" was: "So much story in so little time!"

I am sharing all this information because I hope you will learn from reading and analyzing the screenplay while considering that it is possible to gain recognition for your projects with scarce resources. Remember that the story forms the basis of any good film. You don't need million-dollar budgets, high-tech effects, or a huge crew to make a movie. You need a simple but good idea that you can turn into your own story. Include your crazy ideas and creativity.

Allow your story to become personal.

2

THE PEOPLE

Thanks a lot guys

Without these amazingly talented people, this film would not have happened.
Thanks a lot for your efforts!
Cast:
The Woman: Henriette Steenstrup
The Director: John Brungot
The film crew: Off-screen characters
Crew:
Director, scriptwriter, producer, and editor:
Tomas Sem Løkke-Sørensen
Cinematographer: Even Benestad
Co-editor: Jon Christer Svendsen
Sound recordist: Jørn Ryen
Sound editing: Aksel Holand, Petter Fladeby
Script consultant: Jannicke Systad Jacobsen

3

IMAGE GALLERY

Movie poster

Main character The Actress Wenche played by Henriette Steenstrup

The Director played by John Brungot

The trouble starts!

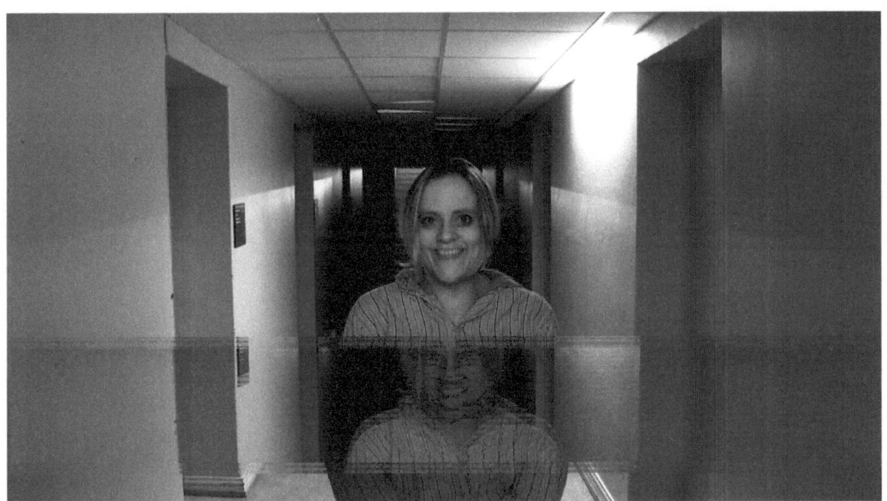

Camera breakdown

4

THE SCRIPT

THE UNHAPPY WOMAN

TomasSorensen©2009

Remember to watch the film after reading the script. Log on to one of these channels: YouTube, Discover Film, Sofy.tv, Filmrommet.no, Filmarkivet.no The easiest way to find the film is to search for **The Unhappy Woman Discover Film** on Youtube.

1. INT. CORRIDOR - EVENING

We see the film from the camera's point
of view. The entire film is filmed in
one camera set up.

A WOMAN stands motionless as she
looks down. She is dressed in a white robe.
She turns her gaze up.

THE WOMAN (artificial)
Jonny, I love you.

She hesitates for a moment then laughs an

exaggerated crazy laugh.

MALE VOICE(OFF)
Cut.

The Woman's laughter stops abruptly.
We see the microphone from the sound
boom as THE DIRECTOR enters the
frame.

THE DIRECTOR
Good, but you're a little tense. A little too
tense. Try to be more natural. Remember
you love Jonny at the same time you hate
him. But otherwise, fine. Okay?

THE WOMAN (ACTRESS) nods.
The Director goes out of frame and behind
the camera.

THE DIRECTOR(OFF)
Okay. Ready for another take?

The picture fades to black.

THE DIRECTOR(OFF)
Oskar, are you ready?

The picture returns.

OSCAR(OFF)
Camera is ready! Camera is running.

SOUND RECORDIST (OFF)
Sound rolling.

The clapper board appears.

CLAPPER LOADER (OFF)
The unhappy woman, take number...

The Actress pushes the clapper board away.

THE ACTRESS
Uh, excuse me. I'm playing a psycho,
right?

THE DIRECTOR(OFF)
Yes.

THE ACTRESS
Then it's a little strange that I should love
Jonny, since psychopaths by definition
can't love…it doesn't seem quite right…

THE DIRECTOR
Um. Don't think about it. But remember
that you've gone crazy because Jonny
has been unfaithful. Okay?

THE ACTRESS
So, I'm not a psychopath anymore, but
morbidly jealous?

THE DIRECTOR
Yes, fine, that's fine. Ready to shoot?
Oskar, is the camera working?

OSCAR(OFF)
Camera is running.

The clapper board comes into frame.

SOUND RECORDIST(OFF)
Sound rolling.

The Actress prepares for another take.

CLAPPER LOADER(OFF)
The unhappy woman, take two.

The clapper board snaps with a bang.

THE DIRECTOR(OFF)
Action.

The Actress looks up.

THE ACTRESS
Jonny, I love you.

She hesitates a little, then starts to cry.

THE DIRECTOR
Cut, cut. Damn. Why are you crying?
You shouldn't cry, you are supposed to
laugh.

He stands in front of her and looks at her
sternly.The picture fades black but comes
back quickly.

THE ACTRESS
It doesn't work for me to laugh now
that I'm not a psychopath anymore. I feel
the jealousy much stronger if I cry.

THE DIRECTOR
What the hell are you doing? Just do
what you're told. Stop acting like a fucking
prima donna.

They stare at each other. The Director
pushes The Actress back into position and
goes behind the camera.

THE DIRECTOR(OFF)
Let's do another take - again.

The clapper board appears.

THE ACTRESS
Prima donna. Damn it, I'll give you prima donna.

She turns and leaves. The Director rushes after her.

THE DIRECTOR
Wenche, come on. I didn't mean it that way. You know very well that you are the only one who can play this role. Don't make trouble...

THE ACTRESS
Yes, exactly. It is quite difficult for me to make a film about adultery with you as a director. You get it, right?

THE DIRECTOR
You must then be able to distinguish between work and private life!

THE ACTRESS
I'm damn well able to tell it apart.

She goes back and gets ready for another take.

THE DIRECTOR
Alright guys, we're getting ready for some filming. Let's keep the good energy here now.

He goes out of frame. We see the clapper board. The Actress stares intently in the direction of The Director

THE ACTRESS
It's just absolutely incredible! I was burnt

out, broken and childless, so you leave me
for that old bitch.

The picture goes black but comes back
seconds later.

THE DIRECTOR(OFF)
Oscar. Is the camera ready?

OSCAR(OFF)
Yes.

THE ACTRESS
What do you want with her? She is the
same age as your mother and looks like a
scarecrow.

THE DIRECTOR (OFF)
Damn Wenche. It's been over three months.
I thought you were over it.

THE ACTRESS
Got over it? We were supposed to start a
family, you and I, but then you just ran
away.

THE DIRECTOR
I was frustrated, okay.

THE ACTRESS
Why? Because of your poor sperm quality?

THE DIRECTOR (OFF)
No, because I didn't love you.

The Actress begins to cry. The Sound
Recordist's hand comes into the frame.
It holds a pack of tissues. The Actress takes
a tissue and wipes her nose.

The Director comes over to her.

THE DIRECTOR
I am sorry...

She begins to cry more intensely.

THE DIRECTOR
Come by on Saturday. I can cook dinner.
Then we can drink some wine and talk
about this...

THE ACTRESS
I don't drink wine.

THE DIRECTOR
No right?

THE ACTRESS
I'm pregnant!

THE DIRECTOR
Pregnant? With whom then?

The Actress hesitates, then she nods weakly
towards the camera, towards one in the film
crew who is behind the camera.

THE DIRECTOR
With Jorn, the sound guy?

THE ACTRESS
No...

She nods more clearly towards the camera
while she stares straight at us.

The Director turns and looks straight into
the camera.

THE DIRECTOR
With Oskar? Damn Oskar, we're best
friends.

He seems at a loss for a few seconds.

THE DIRECTOR
Fuck you Oskar!

He slams the lens straight in, so the picture
starts to blur before fading to black.

Shortly after, the picture returns, still
garbled and indistinct. We glimpse
The Actress.

Slowly she starts to smile. The smile turns
into a monotonous, evil laugh.

THE END

5

WHAT DOES A SCRIPT LOOK LIKE?

Format your script

When handing out your screenplay to distributors, producers, directors, actors, and crew members, you want it to look like it should. Industry professionals expect it to be formatted correctly.

Generally, write your screenplay in the correct font, Courier New, size 12. Start every scene with a numbered heading in capital letters. Underneath the heading, describe the scene visually. When a character says something, make the character's name in capital letters and the character's line in small caps. Consider purchasing a formatting program like Final Draft, or if you are on a limited budget, format the screenplay yourself in Word or Google Docs. I did that for my short film.

Useful online resources on this topic include ScreenCraft and StudioBinder, to name a few. See below how I formatted the screenplay for "The Unhappy Woman."

THE UNHAPPY WOMAN

by Tomas Sem Løkke-Sørensen

Email: agendafilmas@gmail.com
Tel: +47 93041892
TomasSorensen©2009

We see the film from the camera's point of view.
The entire film is filmed in one camera set up.

FADE IN:

1. INT. CORRIDOR - EVENING   1.

A WOMAN stands motionless as she looks down. She is
dressed in a white robe. She turns her gaze up.

                    THE WOMAN (artificial)
          Jonny, I love you.

She hesitates for a moment then laughs an exaggerated
crazy laugh.

                    MALE VOICE(OFF)
          Cut.

The Woman's laughter stops abruptly. We see the microphone
from the sound boom as THE DIRECTOR enters the frame.

                    THE DIRECTOR
          Good, but you're a little tense.
          A little too tense. Try to be more natural.
          Remember you love Jonny at the same time you
          hate him. But otherwise, fine. Okay?

THE WOMAN (ACTRESS) nods. The Director goes out of frame
and behind the camera.

                    THE DIRECTOR(OFF)
          Okay. Ready for another take?

The picture fades to black.

                    THE DIRECTOR(OFF)
          Oskar, are you ready?

The picture returns.

                    OSCAR(OFF)
          Camera is ready! Camera is running.

                    SOUND MAN (OFF)
          Sound rolling.

The clapper board appears.

1.CONTINUED   2.

                         CLAPPER LOADER (OFF)
             The unhappy woman, take number…

The Actress pushes the clapper board away.

                         THE ACTRESS
             Uh, excuse me. I'm playing a psycho, right?

                         THE DIRECTOR(OFF)
             Yes.

                         THE ACTRESS
             Then it's a little strange that I should love
             Jonny, since psychopaths by definition can't
             love...it doesn't seem quite right...

                         THE DIRECTOR
             Um. Don't think about it. But remember that
             you've gone crazy because Jonny has been
             unfaithful. okay?

                         THE ACTRESS
             So, I'm not a psychopath anymore, but morbidly
             jealous?

                         THE DIRECTOR
             Yes, fine, that's fine. Ready to shoot.
             Oskar, is the camera working?

                         OSCAR(OFF)
             Camera is running.

The clapper board comes into frame.

                         SOUND RECORDIST(OFF)
             Sound rolling.

The Actress prepares for another take.

                         CLAPPER LOADER(OFF)
             The unhappy woman, take two.

The clapper board snaps again with a bang.

                         THE DIRECTOR(OFF)
             Action.

The actress looks up.

1.CONTINUED   3.

                    THE ACTRESS
          Jonny, I love you.

She hesitates a little, then starts to cry.

                    THE DIRECTOR
          Cut, cut. Damn. Why are you crying?
          You shouldn't cry, you are supposed to laugh.

He stands in front of her and looks at her sternly.
The picture fades black but comes back quickly.

                    THE ACTRESS
          It doesn't work for me to laugh now that I'm
          not a psychopath anymore. I feel the jealousy
          much stronger if I cry.

                    THE DIRECTOR
          What the hell are you doing? Just do what
          you're told. Stop acting like a fucking prima
          donna.

They stare at each other. The Director pushes The
Actress back into position and goes behind the camera.

                    THE DIRECTOR(OFF)
          Let's do another take - again.

The clapper appears.

                    THE ACTRESS
          Prima donna. Damn it, I'll give you prima
          donna.

She turns and leaves. The director rushes after her.

                    THE DIRECTOR
          Wenche, come on. I didn't mean it that way.
          You know very well that you are the only one
          who can play this role. Don't make trouble...

                    THE ACTRESS
          Yes, exactly. It is quite difficult for me to
          make a film about adultery with you as a
          director. You get it, right?

1.CONTINUED   4.

                    THE DIRECTOR
          You must then be able to distinguish between
          work and private life!

                    THE ACTRESS
          I'm damn well able to tell it apart.

She goes back and gets ready for another take.

                    THE DIRECTOR
          Alright guys, we're getting ready for some
          filming. Let's keep the good energy here now.

He goes out of frame. We see the clapper.

The Actress stares intently in the direction of The
Director (OFF)

                    THE ACTRESS
          It's just absolutely incredible! I was burnt
          out, broken and childless, so you leave me for
          that old bitch...

The image fades to black and comes back.

                    THE DIRECTOR(OFF)
          Oscar. Is the camera ready?

                    OSCAR(OFF)
          Yes.

                    THE ACTRESS
          What do you want with her? She is the same age
          as your mother and looks like a scarecrow.

                    THE DIRECTOR (OFF)
          Damn Wenche. It's been over three months.
          I thought you were over it.

                    THE ACTRESS
          Got over it? We were supposed to start a
          family, you and I, but then you just ran away.

                    THE DIRECTOR
          I was frustrated, okay.

                    THE ACTRESS
Why? Because of your poor sperm quality?

1.CONTINUED   5.

                          THE DIRECTOR(OFF)
              No, because I didn't love you.

The Actress begins to cry. The Sound recordist's hand
comes into the frame. It holds a pack of tissues. The
actress takes on and wipes her nose.

The Director comes over to her.

                          THE DIRECTOR
              I am sorry…

She begins to cry more intensely.

                          THE DIRECTOR
              Come by on Saturday. I can cook dinner. Then
              we can drink some wine and talk about this...

                          THE ACTRESS
              I don't drink wine.

                          THE DIRECTOR
              No right?

                          THE ACTRESS
              I'm pregnant!

                          THE DIRECTOR
              Pregnant? With whom then?

The Actress hesitates, then she nods weakly towards the
camera, towards one in the film crew who is behind the
camera.

                          THE DIRECTOR
              With Jorn, the sound guy?

                          THE ACTRESS
              No...

She nods more clearly towards the camera while she
stares straight at us.

The Director turns and looks straight into the camera.

                          THE DIRECTOR
              With Oskar? Damn Oskar, we're best friends.

The Director seems at a loss for a few seconds.

```
1.CONTINUED                                          6.

                    THE DIRECTOR
              Fuck you Oskar!

He slams the lens straight in, so the image starts to
blur before fading to black.

Shortly after, the image returns, still garbled and
indistinct. We glimpse The Actress.

Slowly she starts to smile. The smile turns into a
monotonous, evil laugh.

THE END.
```

6

WRITING TIPS

There is a lot to consider when you write a movie

Describe your story in such a way so the reader gets a visual idea of what's happening. This rule applies to writing for both short and feature films.Try to avoid loads of dialogue and voiceovers. Film is a visual medium.

<u>Protagonist vs. Antagonist.</u>

The main conflict in your story is the conflict between the protagonist (main character) and the antagonist (main opponent). They might strive for the same goal in the story, but their strategies to win "The Battle" are different because the protagonist and the antagonist have very different sets of values in life. Avoid making your protagonist a good-only character and your antagonist a bad-only character. Remember, like people in real life, they have flaws, fears, doubts, and skills – just like you and me.

Character change is especially important. Your main character must learn something important about life because of the drama in your story. The protagonist should take immoral steps to beat the antagonist and win "The Battle". Example: The protagonist breaks into the antagonist's house to collect evidence against him or her or an organisation in which the main opponent is the leader.

There is no point in having a conflict in your story if it is not motivated. Remember, sometimes both the protagonist and the antagonist are willing to sacrifice other people's lives and their own lives to reach their goal. Strong motives are in play.

Genres

There are several genres to choose from: action, adventure, animation, comedy, crime, drama, experimental, fantasy, historical, horror, musical, romance, science fiction, thriller, war, and western. There are also over 90 sub-genres.

Choosing the right genres for your movie might be difficult, but it is very important to choose the right ones. Don't choose genres because it's "cool" or "awesome." Do an in-depth analysis of your idea to choose the best genres for that particular idea. For a short film, one genre might be enough. But two are better. "The Unhappy Woman" has two genres – comedy and drama. The comedy part is all the clumsiness, with the film crew having great difficulties finishing the take of the film they're making. The drama part is the personal relationship between The Actress and The Director and their backstory.

For a feature, choose two or more genres. E.g., science fiction, drama, and thriller. You must also decide if your idea fits best as a fiction narrative, an experimental piece, or a documentary.

When writing a short film, try to make it simple. Have a single event that develops into the strange and extreme. Avoid including a lot of scenes to make your short a mini-feature – it just doesn't work in that particular format.

Story Structure

When writing narrative fiction, the usual structure of a story is, in simple words, a beginning, a middle, and an ending. Start your script by introducing the world where the story takes place and introducing the characters. The introduction of the protagonist is especially important here. Then, after the inciting event, the protagonist's goal is clearly defined. In the middle, there is an intense ongoing "Battle" between the protagonist and the antagonist, striving for the same goal. In the last part, the climax unfolds. This part is by far the most important event in the story. The climax is the highlight when the protagonist battles the antagonist for the last time to reach the goal. Who wins? Whose moral values will survive and maybe change the world forever? The intensity of the climax must be overwhelming. What does the world look like after the climax? The answer to this question comes during the aftermath. Here, you describe how the characters' lives have changed because of the story and as a result of the climax.

"The Battle" between the protagonist and the antagonist doesn't necessarily have to be physical; it can also be mental – like philosophical or intellectual. It depends on your genre.

Contrast

Remember to include contrast in your story. The characters must differ a lot from each other. The protagonist must be far weaker than the antagonist. This phenomenon will push the protagonist to his or her very limits to win "The Battle." The protagonist must change gradually due to all the trouble caused by the antagonist. When you plot the story, remember that each dramatic event should exceed the previous event – then your story will have a positive dramatic curve.

Watch Movies

One of the best ways to learn the trade of screenwriting is to watch movies and analyze them scene by scene. Learn what works and what doesn't. Watch films you like and films you don't like to explore and reveal the do's and don'ts.

THANKS FOR READING

I hope you liked the book

If you would like updates on my future projects or sign up to become an ARC
Reader, please let me know by sending an email to **agendafilmas(at)gmail.com**
Then, you'll be the first to receive info about upcoming
release dates, book discounts, giveaways, and more!

Your opinion matters!
Please feel free to leave a review of this book on Amazon.
Thanks again.
Best wishes from
Tomas

About the Author

Tomas Sorensen

Tomas is a Norwegian filmmaker and writer. His works have been distributed worldwide and exhibited at top international film festivals such as Aspen Shortsfest, Palm Springs Film Fest, Fantafestival, The Norwegian Short Film Festival in Grimstad, and more. In 2010, Tomas won the Oscar-qualifying Best Short Short Award in Aspen with "The Unhappy Woman."

He is also a big sports and cycling fan. He recently wrote the first Norwegian cycling quiz book, SykkelQuiz (The Cycling Quiz Book), widely distributed in Norway. Tomas is one of the leading cycling experts in his home country.